From the Bone

Poems by Melvin Litton

Kansas City   Spartan Press   Missouri

Spartan Press
Kansas City, Missouri
spartanpresskc.com

Copyright (c) Melvin Litton 2018
First Edition 1 3 5 7 9 10 8 6 4 2
ISBN: 978-1-946642-38-7
LCCN: 2017964753

Design, edits and layout: Jason Ryberg
Cover art: Karl Ramberg
Author photo: Erica Hinter
All rights reserved. No part of this publication may be reproduced or transmitted in any form or by any means, electronic or mechanical, including photocopying, recording or by info retrieval system, without prior written permission from the author.

Spartan Press would like to thank Prospero's Books, The Fellowship of N-finite Jest, The Prospero Institute of Disquieted P/o/e/t/i/c/s, Will Leathem, Tom Wayne, Jeanette Powers, j.d.tulloch, Jason Preu, Mark McClane, Tony Hayden and the whole Osage Arts Community.

Poetic Joust was previously published in *Broadkill Review*, *Waters Still and Green* was previously published in *The Stray Branch*. *One Gothic Eve, The Knobe and Me* and *Waters Still and Green* were previously published in *The Literary Hatchet*.

This little book was very much a birth of chance, and without the keen interest and editing of Jason Ryberg and Spartan Press, it would never be. The cover is by my good friend, Lawrence sculptor-artist-musician, Karl Ramberg – who, as you can see, lifts his images from the stone, while I work my words from the bone ...

CONTENTS

Land of Long Shadows / 1

Catharsis / 3

Spirit Made Flesh / 4

Ja-a-z-z-ed! / 5

Film Noir / 6

Off Work / 7

Curse of Conscience / 8

Down the Woods / 9

Dark Intent / 10

Torque / 11

Gold Rush / 12

The Knobe and Me / 13

Tiananmen Square / 14

Crazy Age Rant / 15

Flight to Paradise / 17

Sister / 20

Son of Mine / 21

Waters Still and Green / 22

Debauched / 23

Hoodwinked / 24

Vampire Breath / 25

Shedding Skins / 26

Faith / 27

Stoned Sober / 28

To Pray / 29

The Willow / 30

Omen / 31

Unearthed / 32

Wry Salvation / 33

Question / 34

Poetic Joust / 35

One Gothic Eve / 36

Chosen Path / 39

The Exile / 40

Sapien or Rapien / 41

Unknown / 42

Harvest / 43

The Gate / 44

The Mountains / 45

, ! ? ... / 46

Moon Dance / 47

Regress of Progress / 48

Prodigal Son / 49

Cigar Smoke / 51

A Prayer / 52

Where Are You, Good Man / 54

Back When / 55

Hard West / 57

Country Singer / 58

Ode to Drunk Bob / 59

The Shepherd Was a Lad / 60

Yes Wind No / 61

Juggernaut / 62

*For my father, Ralph C. Litton
and my mother, Neva Rebecca Bell,
who joined in the flesh long ago
and now share dust and bone...*

Land of Long Shadows

Stand before the setting sun then to the far horizon turn
and face the colors fading from winter's withered sky.
To the land of long shadows
Come.

Walk the bison path over dormant loins of eroding earth,
these subtle swells inter a goddess,
fallen since the age of ice,
fertile on the prairie.

Hear the chantress coyote call, her haunting song
carried on savage winds that scourge and burn the flesh.
Brave the baleful blizzard and like the stunted oak
bow to the earth and her dark warmth ... forbear.

Winter prowls these lonely hills, snow disguised and
hungry, howling bluff to bluff over tufts of grass, brittle,
still, and frozen. Clouds part and lift like smoke from a
dying flame, leaving ashes in the valley.

By the moon's cool light descend the low promontory
and pass beneath the veiling night. Pervade the vast
magnetic ebb and flow where each unnumbered star
is afire with pulsing radiation, crystalline, frost-like ...
yet fusion born, belonging to depths of
ageless nativity.

There, beyond the meager arc of time,
submerged in silence long unbroken ... sleep.

Too soon the sun lifts the veil
from the rim of the coffin earth,
blinding all with light. Awaken!

Snatch the Golden Bough and embrace the huntress
Diana, taste her meat-fed scent and vow to be slain.

To the Land of Long Shadows
Come,
Bear fruit again.

Catharsis

A fifth of vodka and a jackhammer
unleashed the poetry in me — all memory
of rote knowledge, its precise application,
decapitated by the vodka, dead cells
of convention left stomped by
rude rebels of intoxication.
Then the jackhammer
broke my cerebral hymen
and long-checked libido flooded
the parched plains of my primal mind ...

Spirit Made Flesh

Comes a knock at the door ...
Sir, have you thought about Jesus?
Why yes, son, I have ...
I've thought about Jesus standing tall as the clouds
backed by rays of sunlight in the haloed blue ...
I've thought of Jesus dancing fairy rings around a
dandelion, gazing up through yellow petals spread
like boughs of an ancient oak beneath a golden moon ...
And I've sipped thoughts of Jesus slowly through
the straw of a strawberry sundae, thinking
how sweet it is to be saved ...
But as sure as a cow shits manure we all must die,
so mostly I think of my neighbor's young wife,
her angelic blonde hair and soft white skin
calling me down like a fluffed feather pillow
to her hot embrace ...

Ja-a-z-z-ed!

...the trumpet burns its brakes, s-c-r-e-a-m-i-n-g! t-tap ballads of madness...jazz another poppy arm. Behind the mind a traffic siren blazes down an alley, blasting t-tap bullets of my flesh. That bad man on a bench slumped like a broken doll against a wall where spiders crawl as stone ears whisper to the reedy song of a lazy one-eyed saxophone jazzed by the Cyclops Saxon. The Bronze Age laughing, beating drums with wall-splashing rhythms ... as piano teeth snap their own wood ... jazzed from the inside out ... snarling suicide, t-tap badlands of writhing coral snakes, bootleg passions and jazz bees, shapeless figurines in fluid silhouette...picture frames ricocheting from cave to ceiling ... high-wired and falling. Jazz the bones in a pyre, forging resurrection sperm for evil studs. Jazz a new race of embalmed savagery ... dressed in silver spurs for Armageddon. Jazz the pale horse to infernal heaven ... raining hot metal ... a guillotine vocal spiking the ears like lightning dancing on thin ice, opening the bomb-bay to the bowels' last movement, not with a bang or a whimper ... just another poppy arm jazzed. Strung out, hung up, like a hanged man blue-faced in ultra-sonic silence, trumpeting the bleeding flesh through past-tense till the God-made soul is Ja-a-z-z-ed...!

Film Noir

Life never ends like a story complete.
We witness our drama till the film breaks,
as interest wanes and fades, simple as that.
A blank screen, no refund, coiled footage
left in snarls, unedited, tossed to the grave.
We don't die so much as the film just snaps …

Off Work

Driving home, passed a rusted-out
Mustang, its tailpipe dangling like a
donkey's dick tasting the breeze …
Hell, made me laugh, week's end,
I too rolled down my window to lap
the wind, felt like an Egyptian mummy
just unwrapped from a 40-century sleep,
flesh sore and mind numb, awakened like
Frankenstein in want of woman, beer,
and music to light my soul again …

Curse of Conscience

I no longer kill ants.
It may be that ancient notion of karma,
    the timeless oriental spice
    seasoning our cyclical soul,
        has overcome me —

Or, more likely, that old Christian cowardice
    infecting, gutting the self,
    leaving the leper's fear of retribution
        our sole sense of being —

The child, with no compunction,
    smashes bugs by the dozen,
    is not ruled by death,
        but through it rules, whimsically,
        a little god —

But I no longer kill ants,
    no longer have the stomach,
    the freedom or innocence,
        unless they bite me,
        then ... *Smash!*

Down the Woods

Down the woods the dead horse decays
Died of a bullet and a broken leg
Down the woods lies a tall dapple-grey
Always was a stiff-legged ride …

Down the woods with coyotes, birds, and leaves
From dawn to dusk, foul wind, moon and rain
Down the seasons dream-clouds gallop on
Down the woods white bones remain …

Dark Intent

I assault the serious minded as they insult the earth with their scorn for gaiety, these fathers who implore the child with a hornet's nest of words spewing confused hate beneath the clouds … their bitter frost masks a barren fruit, using logic like coiled snakes for paralysis and deception. Like thorns of cactus skin, what use for crippled utterance but paired to a poet's song, this flesh scarred by city pocks, a mass illumined from within, professing to generate a star. Ah go now you silent mischief, the thunder will echo my meaning through a laughing storm, threatening love …

Torque

With anomalous intent I took the slug wrench in hand,
not to repair the lifeless engine so much as to
internalize the tactile experience of elemental
bone, muscle, and sinew at work.

Like a millwright on the moon of generative imagination,
I leapt to the machinating center with shackle, choker,
and chain hoist to lift the massive casing that houses
the secret gearing propelling this life.

But my vision skews, struggling, I squint to focus, to redirect
my twisted schemes skewered on the fine thread of routine.
For I fear they may seat there, hold fast, before my chance
to loosen and escape this terrible torque that
tightens about my throat like a noose.

Gold Rush

With a grubstake from Ohio he went there long ago
Brought a pack mule, a pickax, and a pan to search for gold
Bullet casings, tobacco tins, coffee cans, and bones
Are the remnants left behind his log/sod mountain home
Moss-roofed and fallen now on a high granite slope
Where a lone pine stands sentinel by a dynamite-
cratered hole

Gold! was a booming cry in 1900 or so
Gold was a fever
There was gold in Colorado

But the stillness reigns like starlight
And near a dying patch of snow
Lie the rusting, bleaching remnants
Of bullets, tobacco, coffee, and bones

The Knobe and Me

We haunt the road, the Knobe and me, tread wagon ruts,
   mud, and leaves, past villages where maidens weave,
     down wooded paths that harbor thieves ...
In an enchanted glen I first met the Knobe, a horse
   no larger than a dog, of purest spirit and magic will,
     who laughed when asked, *What is known?*
     and answered simply, *Journey on.*

The pain we witnessed, the joy we shared, the summer
   harvests, the winter lairs, the dark of night, the thrust
   of steel, young soldiers bunched and forced to kill,
     their silhouettes froze against the sky, while
     underfoot we watched them die, the dead
     and maimed in log-jammed streams,
      caulked with red and sodden leaves.

Thus we roamed the Knobe and me, ever fading scene
   to scene, made to journey from child to man through
   a torn, jagged land. Yea, the Knobe and me once
   were young, spry with laughter as songs were sung,
     but the Knobe has saddened and I have aged,
   our world of freedom grown a cage. And no spirit,
will, or manic joy can make a man again a boy.
     Yet the Knobe and I can never part, for we
      share, the man, the beast ... one heart.

Tiananmen Square

(China: The Fourth of June 1988)

From its dark cell in the Forbidden City
The fell beast lunged through Tiananmen Square
To feast on youth's sweet freedom
And banish their tears to air.

While one week later like pity
Rain comes to a parchment land
A world away in Kansas where winds
Mourn the time-blown sand.

Whither their hearts were yearning?
Whether to answer their call?
Free as dust when blood leaves us!
Cry the salt-stained cheeks of the damned.

Crazy Age Rant

Never gone crazy, never quite got there, but I've been just across the border, straddling the fence, non committal. Just turned 36. Somewhat relieved, 'cause I've been 35 for a whole year and they both got that odd number 3…a plum awkward age, I say. Now next year, 37, is odd again, but 3 and 7 add up to 10, so it gets better. And 38, sounds fine, like a pistol shot. Now 39 might be bad, but it's so close to 40 that 40 is what you've got to be concerned with…time like a noose tightening. But hell, I like the 40s all the way through. The 40s announce themselves like you've finally arrived – I'm 40, by God, and it's about time! Then the 40s roll right on up against 50. Now you might think 50, being odd, would bother me, but the 5 is peculiar and more like even 'cause it's half way there, like to ten or a hundred. Say give me a nickel, a fifty, a five hundred dollar bill! Who wouldn't like a five hundred dollar bill? So the 50s, I like … sounds prosperous, gray hair, a fine suit … a gold watch in my pocket. And 60 … well, there's the double 6s waiting … ain't you ever rolled dice? Heading for double 6s should be a thrill, like a gambler's itch for a Royal Flush. Then bingo … 70! Hah! Now three score and ten sounds so cerebral and wise, by then I'll definitely have something worth saying about this life … and, by goll, they better damn well listen 'cause it-just-might-be-the-last-utterance ... our Biblical allotted years and all. But Lord willing, I'll make 80 ... what a wonder? Noble brow, grave, monumental, like Moses. And by 90 she's all mad-crazed, jazz-possessed, full-throttle liberty. Rev up the Harley, Henry, 'cause we're gonna hit a hunnerd! So anyhow, I'm glad I'm no longer 35. Yep, here on out I think I'm gonna enjoy life a whole bunch ...

Flight to Paradise

Thought groups like cloud patterns left behind the jet,
   reflecting in a void above the earth, yet gravity drawn,
     chasing the sun across the waves, heading west
       with the turbulence of invading time zones,
    and far below the ocean…creatures in the darkest depths,
      like demons in the soul, summoned by our passing.
  On a trek to the ashy rim of a volcano… perhaps offend
    the fire goddess and reap a grand eruption spewed
     like hot sperm toward the parting vulva of
       high cumulous into the blue beyond…
     Meanwhile stranded, beached, marooned,
       awaiting an island hop…Aloha!

As night descends on Honolulu my flight ascends for Hilo,
   while endless waves splash ashore at Pearl Harbor
     where one infamous dawn bombs called
   Midwest farm boys to a raging war, their reluctance to
 engage shattered along with two thousand screaming souls.
   What histories of blood-letting lay harbored in Paradise?

Arriving I sleep, wake and explore…towering trees
  escape the lush embrace, fronds anxiously clasp the trunks
    then fall away like discarded lovers to rot and decay.
Bones of rainforest, trunks and broken limbs jut in silent
  agony through pastoral skin grafted like leprosy on
  once virgin land. I walk, wielding my machete against

the dense jungle grass, but the blade prefers the fern.
In a bamboo glen giant staves trap the wind, angry at
their grasp, it battles the fierce foliage for the mist, mist,
the mist … fleeing the rude clatter of ninja bones.

Hurling breakers lash the jagged lava coast, wildly exotic,
yet like a coarse stone, ever honing, sharpening the
ocean's edge. Slopes in precipitous descent meet
imprisoning waves that seem to levitate, the expanse
of ocean rising like a wall of water toward the horizon.
Hawaii, a fern-wreathed isle of volcanic fire and sacrificial
death, an inverted asteroid greened by earth, air, fire, and
water…and I an intruder to the terrain and myth, alien to
custom and dress, doomed to slur the words and reap
native scorn, exchange nervous laughter for their natural
joy as they range the beaches in family clans and friends,
braving the waves, bathing their babes in tidal pools,
teaching them to swim an ocean where only they belong,
while I and others gawk, clumsy, inept, out of place, like
all who've come before…traders, tourists, missionaries,
and with the tides are carried off again.

Nightly mocked by incessant winds and rains knifing
through self and walls, leaving me chill and isolate amid
the savage wail of an ascending tsunami in a fitful dream…
surrounded, harassed, claimed by ghost hands forcing
me to the fateful rim of a deep cauldron…fiery,
vertiginous, spiraling down, damned.

At last the sun shines and a solvent breeze sweeps
   the gray cast from sky and soul upon my descent
      from the emerald forest onto the black lava plain,
     where the sun sips the late evening mist,
    leaving a pale cusped moon eerily suspended
    above the vast shadowed crater of Kilauea Caldera
as the night wind draws a thousand steaming phantoms
    from crevices surrounding Pele's dancing form.

Choral clouds sail above the bay and now and then
    through their amorphous mast and rigging
   appears a lone star yet anchored above Mauna Kea…
     Whereupon I gaze in leaving, my jet
       a silvery sliver in an azure sea…

Sister

Night sky above the old stone church
Stars beyond the moon
Time wrapped in deepest space
Hearts wrapped in a cocoon

When vision breaks this spell
When you cast your dream
Emerge at last with butterfly wings
And escape to where words all fail…

Son of Mine

Son of mine, you were born in a rage,
but soon grew calm in your mother's arms.
Son of mine, I watched you grow a man,
I watched you go to war in a rage-filled land.
And I can never know all the reasons why the heart is torn,
but son of mine, this that we do has been done before
and will be so forevermore ...

Son of mine, when I am gone
you'll cast your shadow where I once stood.
Look to your child and listen to the wind whisper
through the trees and know that life is mostly good.
We can never know all the reasons why the heart is torn,
but son of mine, this that we do has been done before
and will be so forevermore ...

Waters Still and Green

Waters still and green, not of vegetation but of night
and winter ... Umber washes canvas the sky, cradling
fusion's great seed while moon dust descends over waters
still and green.

Lost cities anchor upon the leys and send their women
like mirrored images in dance beyond your reach,
taunting as crows will chide the fields they have cleaned.
You wake besotted and mad, seated cross-legged with
beggars and cads, wishing just once to taste waters
still and green.

Silence, a man-print in the snow, his far voice carries
through the darkness and trees.
Stars needn't guide one whose origins are so near and
terrifying. *My blood is burning!* he cries ... then drinks
from waters still and green.

Debauched

Who is the captain of this ship of fools?
What deep caverns we harbor,
what cruel seas we have sailed…
What great storms have born our laughter…
Neither common black ale nor the poisoned mandrake's
brackish fruit could blind the vision more,
nor set dark gales over the soul half equal to fugues induced
by sirens singing from the lost Isle of Dread Psychos…
Are we like brash Odysseus, madness clothed,
to anchor where each is cursed,
where men are turned to swine by guileful Circe?
By blasphemies bereft of hearth and home?
Our twice-drowned minds lust to mount the Goddess,
at bay in Calypso's cave, we love like dogs…

Hoodwinked

The child is a devout questioner,
its innocence severe and direct.
Our answers serve to maintain our status,
like politicians, we dissimilate and cajole.
The child is lured by clarity masking confusion,
at last trapped by assurances of *ever-after*.

Vampire Breath

How many friends play shades of maudlin life,
vague auras sustained by midnight, fatigue, and wine.
Cratered hearts of borrowed light aglow with lunar deceit,
luring each down wayward paths to meet a greater fire
by half which burns without, yet lays cold within.

Shedding Skins

Cellmates locked in the dungeon night,
our earthly bones of skin, ball and chain,
in cold-blooded bondage we wait to escape
the heartless stone while stars like daggers held
by assassin hands poised and patient as the serpent
waiting for the Gods to whisper *Strike!*

Faith

I believe in the red rose and the matador's cape,
in the bull's madness, the arena and all acts therein.
I believe in fire, the sun, and a young woman's desire
to know passion, the intimacy of night, and the fetal moon.
I believe in the dream and the awakening, that man is
culpable, and that God whispers in a tongue audible solely
to the heart. And I believe in Rembrandt's golden light that
imbues the silent wondrous dust all around and within us…

Stoned Sober

When the weariness of drink overtakes you
and you tire of the barroom din, reflect on the nights
you've wasted in the company of besotted men.
How alike are the faces around you, all accent
their speech with a howl, you and they no better
or worse than a canine pack on the prowl.
So for this were you born a babe and nourished
to be a man, to squint half-blind through the smoke
and like swine sup slop from a hole in a can?

To Pray

At winter's sullen turn
Snow clouds veil the sky
A white so cold can burn
 …the unfurred flesh

Rush to the frail wood
Yet the knife will follow
As the iron mile stands behind
 …a slow whistle

To clasp cool light in cusped palms
Knelt to the straw of boarded myth
To stable my soul in blind calm
 …where vision first saw life

The Willow

The willow breathes to me
From southern winds intoned
Sings to me, *Be calm and patient of the name*
Tis sufficient to know and love the face of things

The willows scents the tides
The olive sweetness of Crimean mystery
Her immobility an omniscient vessel
Of melodious effluvium and sightless imagery
An oriental dance laces her limbs' ballon
Caressing the sleepless self with tales
Of kings, slaves, and all creation

The wind's hot intoxicant stills
And the heart's lucidity abounds
As the willow whispers new phrases
Austere and clear as a winter's eve
In the soft blessing of maternal moonlight

The willows breathes to me
The willow sings to me
Grace is the only glory …

Omen

Thanatos blares his trumpet
As beggar chieftains cross the river
At low tide in the summer season
Their passions drawn taut
Like cactus in drought
Leaving thorns of ragged intent
To thwart the march of straggling innocence

While over the western desert
Sorrow's amorphous clouds blacken
Into a torrent of despair
Charging the blood to seethe and roar
Depositing an angry knowledge too soon imbibed
Alongside the labor and the dream
The call of an awakening suicide
Burning its salt forever through tender wounds

Unearthed

Older than the sharks, down tooth river
we'd crawl through its sand and clay beds
where the sleeping fossils lived when Kansas
was a sea, before the waters placed the shadows
of their flesh upon the cliffs to draw the child's hand
in question of unanswered time, where the secret nibbles
at the riddle and the soft underbelly of clouds harden
into armor-plated storms of assaulting night
like a murderer yet unjudged, unborn …

Wry Salvation

The thief through tragedy gains belief
that a greater hand moves his designs.
Faithless outlaws raid Caesar's realm
and from their bones form Peter's Church,
while the phoenix whore from sin-ash
climbs to brimful love everlasting …

Question

How can this vaporous reality at any given
moment condensed to the rude flesh called self,
if in fact I am the ghost of my father and this world
an illusion whose eternal form is crystalline only in mind,
where is the canvas on which it plays and glows?
What force pervades the execution, are we the artist,
or pigment, or the quintessential goal? My son,
will he invoke my ghost to invest his soul or can he
find his uniqueness sufficient within the phantasmal all?

Poetic Joust

Why allude to the pinion of the linnet's wing, he said,
when brother poets sing of ailerons on sleek silver birds?
Clean riveted verse far outshines archaic rhyme …
I could answer that I have little choice but to prefer such
over airplane noise, that my heart laps from ancient steins
and shares old Bruegel's love of the peasant line …
All this I confess and on my oath I'd shuck new weave
for stout old leather, steal a wench's kiss and plunder art
from arcane cellars rather than bandy, sip, jive and toast …
I'll ride a stallion while you fly snug-belted in coach.

One Gothic Eve

Midnight freezes the mudded wheel to rim
    as winter tolls from its granite tower.
A cowled serf rushes from the cat's cold eye,
    the scythe moon rues the owl's dark hour.
A cottage door bangs lame upon its hinge,
    inside the hearth holds meager warmth
        where lays a child of feeble limb.

The wife stirs thin gruel, her wan eyes cast.
    What have ye to wrap our babe? she asks.
A rag rug front the Bishop's door, says he,
    tendering the gift with frostbit grasp.
She holds it to the flames, feels its thread,
    Hain't had many boot upon it, nay,
        fit to clothe the quick or dead …

From a princely feast the Bishop comes,
    his cape held high o'er the rutted mud
by trailing squire yet his boots be caked
    as he stomps to the door to find no rug.
A thief, I swear! Off now! he cries,
    Fetch Sheriff Red to hang the cur,
        let gibbet crows pluck his eyes …

The Sheriff roused from his warm bed
    curses the news but dons fur coat.
Named the Red for flush heart 'n beard,

he saddles up to hunt the road.
Yonder he spies an old yeoman out
    fetching wood to feed the hearth.
      He reins thereby, firmly shouts:

You there halt! and give true word.
    Hast thou seen nar' one a'prowl
This night 'tween dusk 'n witch's hour?
    Aye, Sheriff Red, m'dog did howl
As John the Sweep did hazard by.
    I know'd him by his limpin' gait.
      He totes a bale…perhaps of rye?

Or wool rug from the Bishop's door…!
    Sheriff Red draws whip and spurs away
and rides to where the Sweep abides.
    He knots his reins at the cottage gate,
storms through the door with wind and sleet.
    All eyes freeze on him standing there,
      'cept babe in mother's arms asleep.

Her eyes plea mercy as the Sheriff points down,
    That rug be the Bishop's, I know it well …
She lowers her gaze in faint appeal,
    Sir, please, John but found it on the trail …
His stern eyes pass from her to the Sweep,
    What say ye, John, you're lookin' pale?
      Has soot clogged yer throat, now speak!

Seated silent, by guilt condemned, John
>nods meekly and answers, *Aye ...*
Aye, you say? Aye? the Sheriff scoffs
>while the baby stirs with fitful cough.
Aye, you found it on the trail, you say.
>*Put there by a timely wind...or hand?*
>>*Now sit you both and both you pray ...*

The woman hugs her babe in fear and weeps
>as Sheriff Red strides out to tethered horse
no doubt to fetch a rope and bind her John
>who hangs his head cursed ... no recourse.
When stout boots return, a blanket he holds,
>*Here, wrap it warm in sweet horse sweat,*
>>*Spare me the rug, yer babe the cold ...*

The Sweep reprieved gives heartfelt sigh
>as she yields the rug and warily asks,
Will ye sit a spell ... by the fire, kind Sir?
>*Have a bit o' soup ... a wee repast?*
Nay, good woman, t'will soon be dawn,
>*and Lord Bishop surely waits anon,*
>>*his precious rug to tramp upon.*

Chosen Path

Today I stand and turn my glance
to all that's gone. To what play or happenstance
do I owe this pivot in life's long journey
that I now should ask
or even wonder at the reflecting glass
that holds my image out of time?
Say the deluge of reverie has come,
dim, overcast, a soul epiphany sprung
via strange pulsing in the blood,
this staid flow through flesh and bone
that's borne, housed, and honed
me these many years, my mold of mud.
A curious denouement…this day I saw
a frost-clothed butterfly fallen in the grass,
still and bent. Then the thawing sun flushed
a frantic mouse that escaped a coiling snake
only to leap in the old cat's maw and end
murdered in the shadow of the house.
A man's allotted three score and ten,
and half my years now sadly gone.
I hunger for youth … passions fading
like lush autumn colors to wintery gray.
Will I escape the coils of folly only to serve
as cruel repast, the predator grown prey at last …?

The Exile

I will rise from these icy waters
And gather the wind about me
In crave of hot liquors and wine
As the sun dreams my fields
And not worry of the winter's haunting
For a basketful of summer harvest
Awaits the end of my journey …
I'll drive my thumbs into the clever soil
To procure the quickened fruit
And from a tiny seed and earth womb
I'll squeeze sweet juices and cleanse
The hunger from my soul … storm waters
Will wash and free me of the hopeless dead
And an autumn tavern will cradle me
As the nest its egg … then I shall open and fly
Through the heavens I have known …
Hear me I am the crow against the cloud
The voice hidden in the river
Forgotten are my wanderings my longing and debt
Sufficient are my savings to gain passage home …

Sapien or Rapien

We search the mysteries of the world
and our being like mad fools trying to discover
the workings of a motor with a cutting torch …
The web torn, the heart stopped, feathers stuffed,
every surface and interior altered by the manner
of our touching … our best tools, like flint knives,
butcher the beast yet slay the fine edge of its mystery.
The primitive looked upon the night sky and saw
the face of God and heard him speak while
we delve into that night with radio-telescopes,
hear thermonuclear rumblings and know him not.
Wonder at the faithless vanity of Narcissus
scanning the firmament not out of love
or understanding but for his mirror image …

Unknown

Perhaps the secret of life lies compressed
in veins of marble on some far mountain range,
or entombed in the dark decay of a remote jungle,
maybe it orbits with the moons of Jupiter,
or drifts capsuled in galactic mists
light-years beyond imagining
like an embryonic wish,
dreamed of, yet unspoken …

Harvest

Born out on those vast plains, set down
in a lonely landscape like the last electron
beyond which matter shrinks into the void,
yet for a time spared and cradled by family …
Of my first memories I nap on a gunny sack
lain over a wheat-stubble mattress, curled up
against a crock jar filled with cistern water
to slake the dust-cough and chaff-thirst in
my father's throat, his face blistered by
tractor exhaust as he nudges the yellow
CAT pulling the combine's sickle and reel
over a sun-bleached field of ripened wheat …
I was brand-new that day, fresh as winnowed
straw, pure as the flame from a blue-tip match
that would soon fire and blacken that golden mane
and prepare the earth, then us all, to receive the plow.

The Gate

An abandoned homestead, the house
and outbuildings now vanquished, returned
to the soil, covered with grass. Several fruit trees,
a lilac, and a tilted cedar stand remnant of those
who once laughed, worked, and cried within …
A metal gate clangs against a post like a
stern ghost barring entrance while the
wind gains voice through the trees,
vague and distant. No matter how
long you ponder, the past cannot be
claimed, nor the present stilled, though
you may lay close to the ground and listen …

The Mountains

In the darkest night behind the walled
    summits and rush of stars …
  my sleep awakens to torrents of
    wind through trees relaying
      a stark intimacy of spirit …

The mountains, they were here before
    and will be here long after …
  and what we sense from their presence,
    in the confused pulse of our blood,
      is that they will own our bones …

, ! ? ...

Born tiny, our feet tucked under
like a comma, deeply embedded,
with all yet to come. Then we grow
tall and straight in quest to jump free
like an exclamation and shout our name!
Slowly through the years we bend,
part in longing to return to our roots,
part in wonder if there is nothing more.
Does all simply end with a period?
Or is that period perhaps a seed to
form again ... tiny, feet tucked under,
deeply embedded in the soul of further tale ...

Moon Dance

I dance for the moon
The moon sings my shadow
Swells with song like a wind-filled sail
Together we laugh reflecting the sun
Long ago moonchild and mother
A ripple on the timeless sea
I dance for the moon
She sings my shadow …

Regress of Progress

Once to cross a river required
courage, faith, and daring,
now we span the waters
through arrogance of engineering.
The etchings of draftsmen void of beauty's line
while the Word depicts mere specification of design,
and old warriors yield to managerial elites who use
math to plunder as drones blindly serve the Beast.

Like the bee's twice embezzled fruit,
from sun through flower wrested,
we quarry both poles and the Seven Seas
with power usurped from God invested.
A devious veil obscures our understanding,
we perceive obliquely, our experience tangent,
and grope forever to grasp an essence
whose center is elusive as lost branches.

Prodigal Son

Now a man at his father's grave
Yet still the child the day he died
He stares at the obscure stone
Seizing on old forms, beliefs
Expecting force and pregnancy
Peeking through a keyhole at death

Through cities he had gazed
Down aisles of towering tombs
Amid clamor of steel and glittering glass
Where Sirens pickpocket every room
And Gargoyles perch from arches
Watching cats and demons mate
While men caterwaul door to door

In harbors where lost sailors port
He anchored his drunken boat
Mooring as the moon on the sea
To prowl among the Demimondes
Twirling neon whips and laughter as
Railroad bulls, challenging and steamful,
Mounted freight loads of comely coal
Brutish, broad, and maddening

His heart ticked and pulsed to
Junk-clocks of the Renaissance
Tolling from cradle to the grave
And like in the old lullaby
He fell from perilous treetops
Somersaulting through night and day
Learning that swift currents run shallow
Still waters run deep

Shedding skin he returns to fire
A cap-gun over his father's bones
In hard regret as soldiers do
Crying in echo of a forfeit life
A longing, a pain uncoiled
Waiting like the Little Prince
To be bitten and taken home again …

Cigar Smoke

An ethereal blue in the sunlight
flowered of earth brown and white ash
borne off in the wind with thoughts
of mortality and crushed dreams
all stubbed out at the chewed end …

A Prayer

Once ... as a small child
   an old bachelor name of Tom Hiney
   gave me a goat to love ...
   My father said it was a good goat
   as did my mother and sisters and brother.
   I fed the goat on cow's milk
   but he died and I was stricken.

Life passed ... I played the days,
   sang of prairies, and dreamt often.
   Roy Naylor our neighbor back then
   held me on his lap one day
   and let me view through his field glasses ...
   my world loomed larger than ever
   and I was amazed.

Yes ... and I learned to walk at the heels of men
   and listen to them talk of the weather and other years.
   My father often walked with Earl McKamin
   and I would follow for Earl rolled his own
   and he'd toss one to the ground half smoked
   I'd snatch it up, rush behind the outhouse
   and smoke it down ... it seemed good to me.

No … nor do I forget one sorrowful day
  I was six years old …
  That day saw my father dead
  and I was stricken.
  Next day I found his hat
  and held it close for the longest time
  for it smelt of him.

Now … the years are many that have gone
  I am a sad, joyous, angry young man.
  I too roll my own and toss them
  to the ground half smoked and
  talk wisely of life with other men and
  wear a hat which sometimes smells of him
  when I work and wipe the sweat from my brow.
  I have found a good woman
  and she has given me a son to love …
  We feed him on cow's milk
  and I pray he lives well.

Where Are You, Good Man

So you're here, are you …?
But where is here when here is
viewed from the roof of your house?
And where's your house from
the highest building in the city?
Can you see anything of this city
from the moon … and does the moon shine
so big as to be seen from the farthest star?
Now, where are you, good man,
are you not lost too …?

Back When

Back when the sky was high, back when
I'd catch up a bull-snake by the tail
and snap him around my head
just to hear him spit then send him spinnin',
flippin', hissin' angrily into a coil, back when

I'd sing my songs loud and full
so's anyone could hear and I was proud
for they was all my own, back when

I'd look as far as I could see
then run and run till I got there
and cry and scream *Whoo-peee!!*
just like an Indian, back when

I could hear the roarin', poundin' splash
of Niagara Falls by just pissin' and
when I'd fart the thunder would echo me
and I thought I just caused a wild tornado
to go tearin' across the prairies, back when

I'd look into a mirror, throw back my chin,
point my finger there and say,
Hey, there you are, back when

I talked tongue-in-cheek with mighty Kings
and fought in every battle like as not
and shared grave secrets with my God
and crossed my heart and hoped to die, back when

What I wanted to be, I was ...

Hard West

Scarred by Dakota winds and dead-end roads,
where hundred-car freights of loaded coal pass
ghost farms, graves, and pasture bones,
where a redhead mourns her road-killed man
in midnight bars with one-night stands,
and an old hombre rides alone at
night in answer to el coyote's cry,
where the blues still hatch them old
refrains of murder, lust, and winter rains ...
Beneath the dust lays ocean rock
and above the land an endless sky,
where shadows labor to the sun
in thirst for water, oil, and love till
even a damn fool's gotta know
he's been fishin' in the wrong hole ...
But hit town at sundown, cast regret away
on whiskey, bets, and naked sweat in chance
for a better day ... as night deepens, cars wreck,
lives too in haste and ruin...with bare hands
you grip the wheel on a rutted road to
the distant hills where all is given and all
is blest, face another sunrise in the Hard West ...

Country Singer

I'm a creek-bank-ghetto boy, a two-legged child of the
prairie. I been blown between the Rockies and the
Rising Sun, and I've tumbled up against a few cities.
I began my singin' on the northern tip of the
Louisiana Purchase, along the night shores of
Edmonton, Alberta. I stayed the whiskey season then
caught a warm southeasterly. I've touched Canada,
the North Atlantic, and mined Colorado all over;
I found that Kansas has the softest loins. The military
trained me to stand upright and I've worked a pick-ax
and shoveled my grave a thousand times. The booze
has begun to line my face. I've got an opinion on
everything and I'll sing till I'm hoarse or the stalls
are empty. I consider myself a neo-pagan, a bat-winged
balladeer. The earth is my totem and I hold by her and
all her species. I fly the banner of the Dagger and the
Rose and declare my faith in both; all this is in my songs.
The Shepherd of Wolves, moon-mad and musical,
I ain't no socialist jukebox. Mostly I bat my own pitches,
though I'll hit an occasional Jimmie Rodger's spitter,
the Hank William's slow ball, and that Bob Dylan slider.
I'm traditional enough to walk some pretty ballad
and mean enough to go down swingin' against
the knuckle ball …

Ode to Drunk Bob

Do you see the silhouette against the sky?
Everyone's laughing … do you see?
The silhouette against the sky, it's Drunk Bob,
everyone's laughing …
See his hands … they hang like wet socks from his arms,
and his mouth gapes like a panting dog without a tongue …
There, see … he's the silhouette against the sky,
everyone's laughing …
Watch Drunk Bob, listen,
Gawd it's hard bein' straight …
panting to the distance he howls,
Yieee-A-A-AH … hurry sundown!

The Shepherd Was a Lad

In many a sleep, O stealing song, I caressed and
played my heart as one would knead a hill to rise …
Wine, the leaven of my days and Lo! I could breed
till morning's gone, in many a sleep, O stealing song …

After I have shipped the pasture down and lain my lambs
to rest, O Dawn! Forgetting as the frigate sails whence were
East or West…then dusk and hunger, ravenous lust, and O if I
could touch her gown after I have shipped the pasture down…

To die, to die, is false you know … Old Landor once spoke
to me, When women moan the waning moon we must give
their tears our chest and lay them swooning and draw them
in, for ours is life when we have sown, *To die, to die, is false
you know …*

Through the dark clouds nightly born, O sweet the vision
Of the woman beast, this creature masked and deathly came
to woo my pleasure through claw and fang, as heat is fusion,
our love was storm, through the dark clouds nightly born …

In the golden of the grain nestled nectars of the rain, I pull the
day closely round as the she-wolf threatens then lay my hand
upon her breast, I give her song, I give her lamb, no greed, I
leave the wolf unchained…in the golden of the grain nestled
nectars of the rain …

Yes Wind No

A sighing whistle plays through the wind
to my ears ... I question, *What is calling?*
How suddenly slow I scan re-memory's gaze ...

Whether when I's three and running with
ol' Rover, or thirteen and hunting squirrel,
or twenty clutched in passion, or when later,
smoking alone, the wind has carried this notion,
whether breezing young or blowing old,
that for one grass-blade moment I've known
the Secret Tale all told, and the next I know none ...

Then I laugh and whisper, *So?*
slake my vision and squint around me,
wondering vaguely of passings by ...
Yes wind no ... all now stilled
to my ears ... yet what was calling?
How suddenly slow I scan re-memory's gaze ...

Juggernaut

Barefoot…I found myself a path that led to a little candle flame. Then the greater darkness that had cornered the dawn yielded to the vast road of morning's gilded dust. And only the little darkness remained beneath my hat brim, it's shade, my only solace from the sun.

Genesis…as a child I set the sundial and sailed the river, seas, and oceans of the sun, and no shadow cast across the granite face, a timeless voyage, that of the ghost prince and his princess. Then a priest appeared and breathed his vision …

The flame was first a thought, he said, before it was the sun. As flesh was first a shadow before it had existence … as void is the eternal measure of all. But, I cried, am I only dream and not flesh? A ship must have a hull to cleave the waters. If sail and sail only I would fall like a tailless kite before the wind? Ah now, child, he countered softly, is not the surface that buoys the vessel not the vessel's shadow? One must hoist the sail and journey on. Consider, what does not grow, must die. For a seed is meant to flower and fructify, its progeny infinite as only god could divine its limits. And has he divined ours? — He has. Is this not paradox? — Yes … and the seed which has born each and all else …

I have grown and rested now and call my neighbor by a whistled tune, but seems I am yet early, so will only draw refreshment from his cistern's depth then on the path and no disturbance make. The rooster crows triumphant for the night was safe for fowl. Today some wolf sleeps hungry.

Yet I walk and do not recall my waking ...

A wish ... I have known the spans of bridges, known them by my palms, bled concrete sutures about my wounds that I may continue on the road, counting telephone poles and envying their lengths for my cabin.

I met two gravediggers along the way and asked of what they buried. *Why sir,* they answered, *we but sift the dust ...*

Such a joyless land ... I have known her width and breadth and still am empty. A carnival of tears ... a festival. Clowns were once a mystery in their makeup, toting baggage made of leather. The circus came by train. And the men who drove the spikes with arm and hammer, who had laid the tracks and later built the big top ... paused and laughed, noting the ladies about town. Great strong men with lathered sweat upon their faces, their jerky came between the flames of two flesh-burning deserts, the sun and hell's hot earthly labor.

I once had a fine young sweetheart, we often walked
in search of daisies, but the day's warm odors usually
led to brier thistles instead. Now I am older and choose
my ladies for the flush in their cheeks and not how
clean their linen.

O Star Lady! No longer my mistress, robed in cold
bronze, and the phantom flame once held high to light
my path, sheds a lifeless gaze. Were you not my
princess liberty when we sailed the timeless ocean?

O Star Lady … soiled and flameless beacon …

Forsaken, I walked the rails, steel threads bespeaking
a time when our grandfathers, their horses, plows,
and women, tended the land. That focus and dimness
called heritage, dirt roads and weathered planks,
greeting cards of lost generations and ghost towns,
an uncharted prism of ruin and distorted memory …
the wilderness of our spirit. I walked the railroad,
following its drift, for I was weary of my time and
longed for an old music made new…Jazz, Dixieland
or Rock 'n Roll, anything with a trace of blues.
I journeyed to the railroad's terminus and found no
music, only a dark brick jungle of stench and rubble
and a million workers attending a dilapidated metal man.
He had a cast-iron casing for a skull and an aluminum
skeletal frame piping machine oil to his rusted pain.

Other frictions wore him down, but a molten cinder
cough fueled the crisis. They transplanted a human
heart which the tin man rejected. Yet he heaved anew,
and the first word he spoke was *On*. Then a keen computer
brain, and still the only word he spoke was *On*.
They gathered round and shouted *Hurrah!* to their grand
behemoth, their analytical totem of digital-arithmetic
ancestry. They worshiped electricity as the second coming.
And the last word the tin man spoke was *Off*.
His rust spread out over the land, extending to bi-ways
and junkyards. His legs and arms no longer moved as
the gearing and struts loosened, sinking away like
dinosaur bones in old river clay.

O Star Lady! America is no longer a dream, it's a job.
The houses built so that within a year
they look like last year's toys. Upon the broken boats,
bottles, and sleepless beds, broken glass
and rusted nails, the industrial barnacles breed.

O Star Lady! Cast those golden slippers onto my path
so I may avoid such perils as stickers and snails and
the devil's claw now dragging at my ankles.

I walked to the day's littoral along the night's masked sea
to search the bars where sailors and whores had harbored,
for I had heard that within that beery realm resides
the poet's library.

I entered as an old drunk proclaimed, *There's nothing
out there, boys, but the grave. That's all is waiting.*
And I said, *Sure, old man, but you'll never make it from
there to now.* He stood and roared, *Don't tell me of
paradox, boy! Damn, I've had it up to my ears!
I've lived to see my betters fall, so I know a thing or two!*

I delivered him my reach and matched him in draughts
of ale as we danced upon the stools and countertops.
Then the old geezer sang his prophet's toast: *To health,
my lads, and loony tunes! And beware they who pose as
leaders and guides to the spirit, for most are merely base
destroyers of the flesh!* As he gasped to speak once more,
I saw in his red eyes the priest from my childhood.
We walk, he said, *with our backs to a cold wind, and what
we think is the future is the past fading into the distance.
We step blindly till fate falls like a hammer blow to the
back of our heads! Hah!*

We laughed and cried and drank it to the last, then
shipped ourselves into the street. We dubbed our vessel
the *Juggernaut* and set sail singing old ballads and
minstrel hymns to sagas of lost homelands, women,
and grief ... A million fey, tragic souls coalesced
and joined in the fugue.

I found myself divided from the people, alone,
undelivered. I walked the night's dark prism as phantom
cries lashed my face. Spirits of the hills arose and
followed. I walked the agonies of my father's sleep.

Yet I caught a hint of laughter in the sky, a pinch of salt, for I had still a pint of fermented gold streams in my stomach flask, and in my vest a railroad watch which timed the moon's egress across the sky.

I walked from sleep to wakefulness, my unburdened passage laughter sired. Spat the whiskey-bred seed to the cloddy earth then fell as a skeleton of old shovels, rakes, and hoes into a grave where hands displaced matter which minds can never form.

And through the clouds the night-wolf hiatus screamed a broken hole, where the moon once had shone, and now only large feathers filtered off the black raven sky. Then a single yellow bird flew in from there, and a million score soon followed, singing ... and chasing the raven from my land.

Melvin Litton's stories have appeared in *Mobius, Foliate Oak, Floyd County Moonshine, Pif, Chiron Review, First Intensity,* with poetry in *Broadkill Review* and *The Stray Branch*. He has two published novels: *Geminga,* a man/raven fable concerning the Shining Path in Peru (III Publishing, 1993); and *I, Joaquin,* a fictional memoir of the Gold Rush bandit, Joaquin Murrieta, as told by his head encased in alcohol (Creative Arts Book Co., 2003) — both available in new editions from Crossroad Press. He is a retired carpenter and lives in Lawrence, KS with his wife Debra and their black and tan shepherd Jack. He also writes and performs songs solo and with the Border Band:www.borderband.com

This project was made possible, in part, by generous support from the Osage Arts Community.

Osage Arts Community provides temporary time, space and support for the creation of new artistic works in a retreat format, serving creative people of all kinds — visual artists, composers, poets, fiction and nonfiction writers. Located on a 152-acre farm in an isolated rural mountainside setting in Central Missouri and bordered by ¾ of a mile of the Gasconade River, OAC provides residencies to those working alone, as well as welcoming collaborative teams, offering living space and workspace in a country environment to emerging and mid-career artists. For more information, visit us at www.oac.com

Osage Arts Community

www.ingramcontent.com/pod-product-compliance
Lightning Source LLC
Chambersburg PA
CBHW021448080526
44588CB00009B/748